This book belongs to _____

Age _____

Favourite player _____

Prediction of Burnley's final position this season _____

Prediction of Premier League winners this season _____

Prediction of FA Cup winners this season _____

Prediction of EFL Cup winners this season _____

Prediction of teams to be relegated from the Premier League this season:

18th _____

19th _____

20th _____

Written by twocan

Contributors:
Rob Mason & Peter Rogers

A TWOCAN PUBLICATION

©2016. Published by twocan under licence from Burnley FC.

Every effort has been made to ensure the accuracy of information within this publication but the publishers cannot be held responsible for any errors or omissions.

Views expressed are those of the author and do not necessarily represent those of the publishers or the football club.

All rights reserved.

ISBN 978-1-909872-81-3

PICTURE CREDITS
Press Association,
Action Images,
& Andy Ford

£8

4

CONTENTS

Champions 2015/16	06
The Squad 2016/17	08
Tom Heaton Poster	18
Spot the Season	19
On Our Way!	20
Here We Go!	22
Skills: Cruyff Turn	24
Sam Vokes Poster	25
A-Z of the Premier League · Part 1	26
Pre-Season Training	28
Andre Gray Poster	30
On the Road	31
Danger Men	32
Design a New Kit	36
Scott Arfield Poster	37
Who are yer?	38
Dream Team	40
Johann Berg Gudmundsson Poster	42
Spot the Season	43
A-Z of the Premier League · Part 2	44
Skills: Rainbow Kick	46
Michael Keane Poster	47
Fantastic	48
Wonder Kid	50
Goal of the Season	51
Spot the Season	52
Jeff Hendrick Poster	53
Players' Player of the Year	54
What Ball?	55
Club or Country?	56
Hat-trick Heroes	57
Skills: Maradona Spin	58
Steven Defour Poster	59
2016/17 Predictions	60
Answers	62

CHAMPIONS

2015/16

SQUAD 2016/17

Tom HEATON — 01

Position: Goalkeeper **Nationality:** English **DOB:** 15.04.86

Heaton played an integral role in Burnley's journey to the Premier League and 2016/17 sees him retain the captain's armband. This summer he became the first Clarets player since Martin Dobson in 1974 to earn a full England cap.

Matthew LOWTON — 02

Position: Defender **Nationality:** English **DOB:** 09.06.89

Last season was Lowton's first at Turf Moor and after recovering from a niggle picked up in pre-season he made his first start for the Clarets in December 2015. He remained a regular, helping Burnley to the top of the Championship.

Jon FLANAGAN | 04

Position: Defender **Nationality:** English **DOB:** 21.01.93

Liverpool defender Flanagan signed on a season-long loan in August 2016. The versatile full-back is one of the most promising talents to emerge from the Reds' Academy in recent years.

Michael KEANE | 05

Position: Defender **Nationality:** English **DOB:** 11.01.93

Keane played all but one league fixture in the 2015/16 Championship title-winning campaign, scoring five goals, two of which were vital last minute equalisers against Brighton and Middlesbrough.

Ben
MEE
06

Position: Defender **Nationality:** English **DOB:** 21.09.89

Mee produced excellent performances last season and played an integral part of a defence that remained unbeaten for 23 league games. He impressed his peers and was crowned Player's Player of the Season.

Andre
GRAY
07

Position: Striker **Nationality:** English **DOB:** 26.06.91

2015/16 was Gray's debut season for the Clarets, he finished the campaign with 25 goals and was crowned the league's top scorer! He scored his first Football League hat-trick in December 2015 against Bristol City.

Sam
VOKES
09

Position: Striker **Nationality:** Welsh **DOB:** 21.10.89

Vokes scored the goal that earned Burnley promotion in May 2016. He then became the first Burnley player to score at a European Championship finals, when he scored for Wales against Belgium in France.

Dean
MARNEY
08

Position: Midfielder **Nationality:** English **DOB:** 31.01.84

Marney has suffered with injury in recent seasons but the 2015/16 campaign saw him make his 200th appearance for the Clarets as Sean Dyche's side were promoted as Champions!

Ashley BARNES | 10

Position: Striker **Nationality:** English **DOB:** 30.10.89

A knee injury ruled Barnes out for most of the 2015/16 campaign. However, he did return to the Clarets side against former employers Brighton in April, before starting in the 2-1 victory away at Birmingham City.

Jeff HENDRICK | 13

Position: Midfielder **Nationality:** Irish **DOB:** 31.01.92

A firm favourite at Derby last season, Hendrick joined Burnley for a club-record undisclosed fee this summer. He recently landed the Republic of Ireland Young Player of the Year award and impressed at the Euros.

Michael KIGHTLY | 11

Position: Midfielder **Nationality:** English **DOB:** 24.01.86

A former England U21 winger, Kightly made the permanent switch to Burnley in 2014. A valuable squad member last season, he made 21 appearances in all competitions, contributing two assists.

Patrick BAMFORD | 15

Position: Striker **Nationality:** English **DOB:** 05.09.93

Chelsea striker Bamford joined on a season-long loan in August 2016. In the 2014/15 campaign, Bamford scored 17 times in 38 Sky Bet Championship games and went on to be named the divisional Player of the Year.

Steven DEFOUR | 16

Position: Midfielder **Nationality:** Belgian **DOB:** 15.04.88

Defour joined the Clarets in August 2016 for a club-record undisclosed fee. He comes with a sizeable pedigree, having been capped 46 times for Belgium and winning the domestic league title twice during his time at Standard Liege.

Paul ROBINSON 17

Position: Goalkeeper **Nationality:** English **DOB:** 15.10.79

A vastly experienced goalkeeper, Robinson joined the Clarets on a free transfer in January 2016 providing back-up for Tom Heaton. He is also a former England international with 41 caps.

Stephen WARD 23

Position: Defender **Nationality:** Irish **DOB:** 20.08.85

A Republic of Ireland international, Ward broke into the side in December 2015 and never looked back. He made 27 appearances in total last season, helping to keep 20 clean sheets in a watertight defence.

George BOYD 21

Position: Striker **Nationality:** Scottish **DOB:** 02.10.85

A tireless midfielder, Boyd joined the Clarets in August 2014 and has since established himself as a firm fans' favourite. He proved an integral part of the team last season scoring 5 goals and registering 5 assists.

Johann Berg GUDMUNDSSON — 25

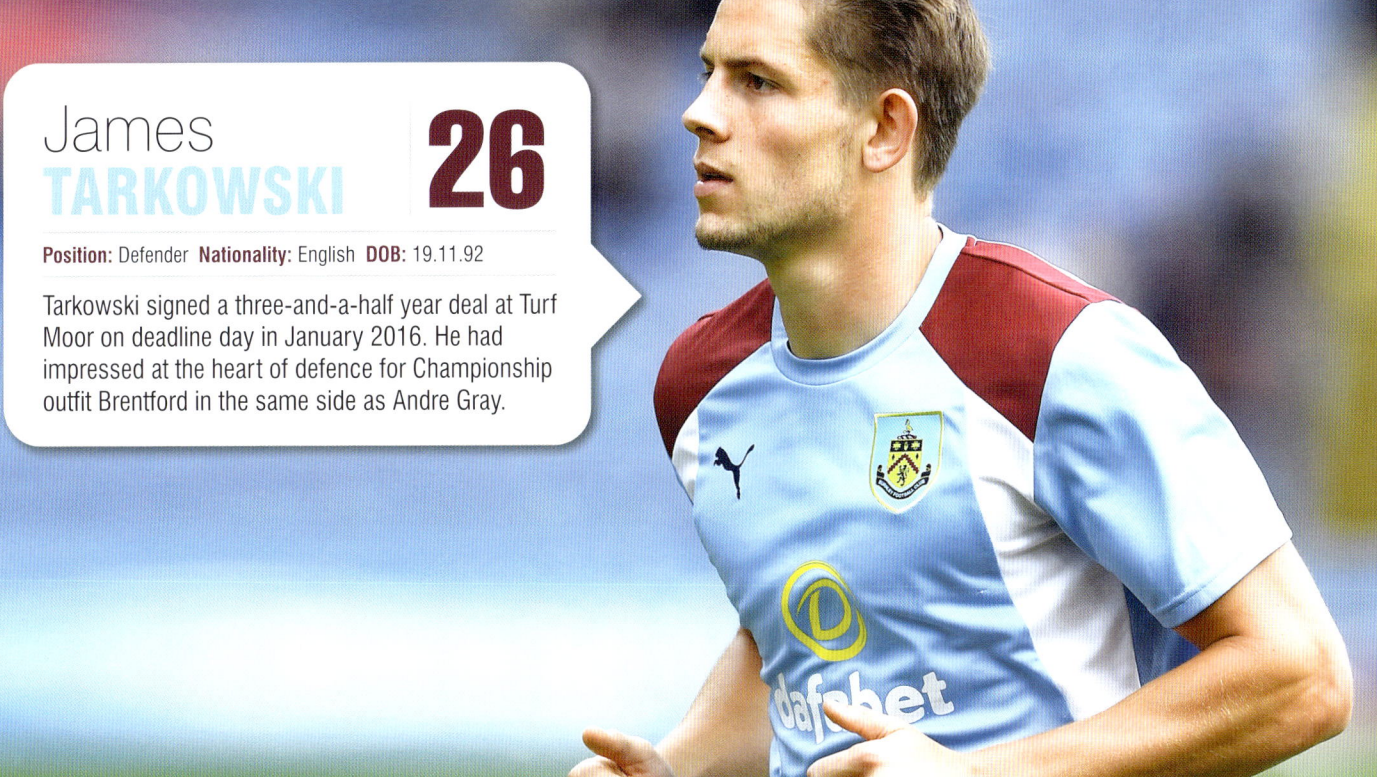

Position: Midfielder **Nationality:** Icelandic **DOB:** 27.10.90

Burnley signed Gudmundsson on a three-year deal from Charlton Athletic this summer. The wide man has earned over 50 caps for his country and in 2013 became the first Iceland player in 13 years to score a hat-trick.

James TARKOWSKI — 26

Position: Defender **Nationality:** English **DOB:** 19.11.92

Tarkowski signed a three-and-a-half year deal at Turf Moor on deadline day in January 2016. He had impressed at the heart of defence for Championship outfit Brentford in the same side as Andre Gray.

Tendayi DARIKWA — 27

Position: Defender **Nationality:** English **DOB:** 13.12.91

Darikwa made his full Clarets debut away at Leeds last season, providing the assist for Vokes' leveller in the 1-1 draw. He continued to impress, making 24 appearances and scoring his first goal at Championship level against Reading.

Nick POPE — 29

Position: Goalkeeper **Nationality:** English **DOB:** 19.04.92

Pope arrived at Turf Moor on the same day as Charlton teammate Gudmundsson this summer. He made 28 appearances for the Addicks last term including the last day of the season where Burnley clinched the title.

Kevin LONG — 28

Position: Defender **Nationality:** Irish **DOB:** 18.08.90

A highly-rated defender, Long who joined the Clarets from League of Ireland side Cork City back in 2010. He gained valuable experience last season with loan spells at MK Dons and Barnsley.

Scott ARFIELD — 37

Position: Midfielder **Nationality:** Scottish **DOB:** 01.11.88

Arfield was an ever-present last season, starting all 46 Championship games and scoring eight times, including stunning efforts at Blackburn and Brentford. He received a well-deserved international call-up for Canada in March.

Aiden O'NEILL — 41

Position: Midfielder **Nationality:** Australian **DOB:** 04.07.98

O'Neill previously played for Brisbane Athletic before making the trip to England. He signed his first pro deal in January 2016, and made his Premier League debut as a substitute against Liverpool in August 2016.

Tom Heaton

01

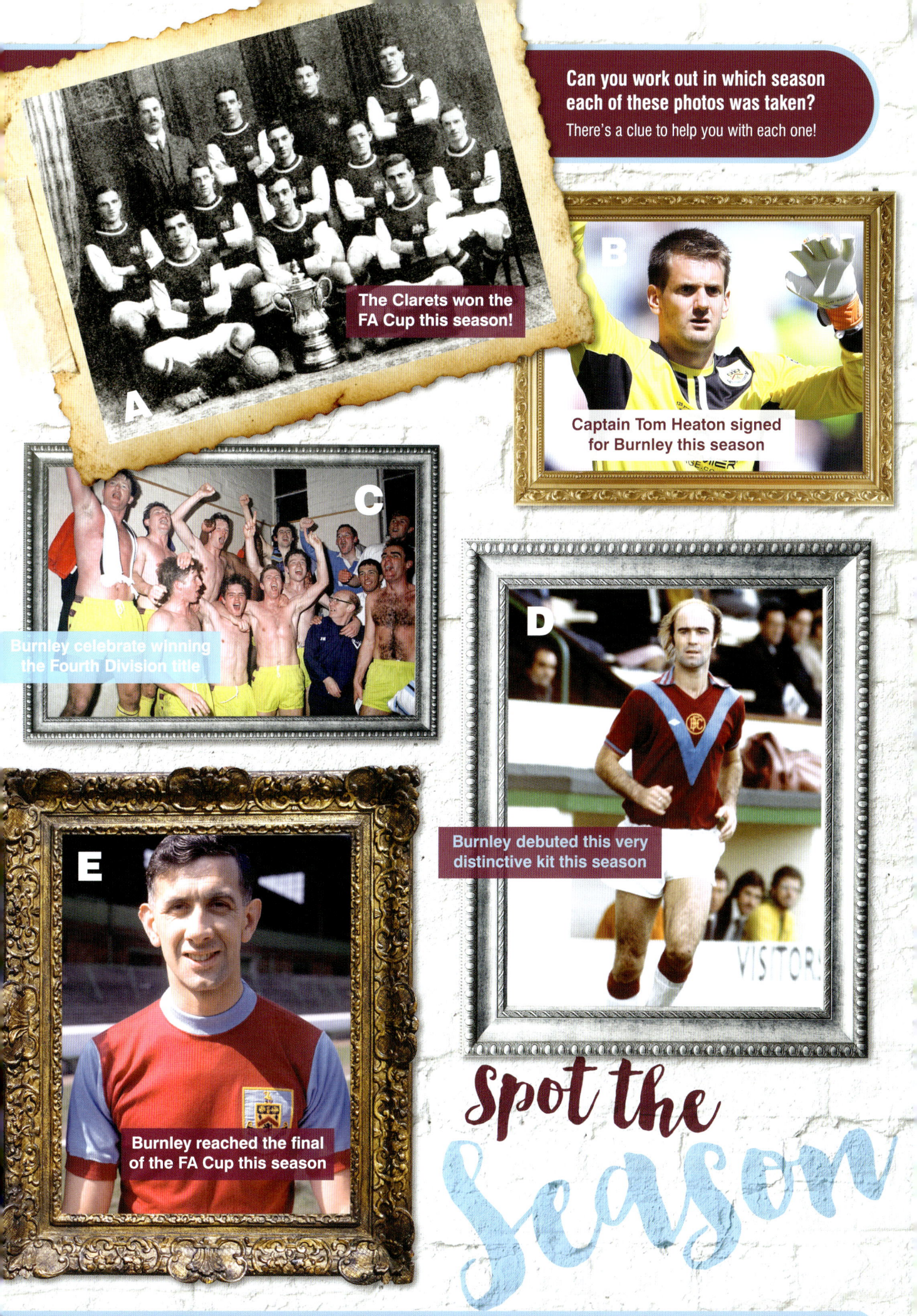

Can you work out in which season each of these photos was taken?
There's a clue to help you with each one!

A — The Clarets won the FA Cup this season!

B — Captain Tom Heaton signed for Burnley this season

C — Burnley celebrate winning the Fourth Division title

D — Burnley debuted this very distinctive kit this season

E — Burnley reached the final of the FA Cup this season

Spot the Season

ANSWERS ON PAGE 62

ON OUR WAY!

Two points from the first four games, including a League Cup elimination, didn't augur well as Burnley looked for an instant return to the Premier League, but things would soon improve. A run of four successive victories was was broken by a draw and a defeat, but the response was to go nine unbeaten. This was followed by a sticky patch of four points from five games up to Boxing Day, but the 4-0 home thrashing of Bristol City two days later was the start of a spectacular run which would not see the Clarets suffer another league defeat all season!

16 victories and seven draws represented an unbelievably magnificent second half of the campaign as Burnley bounced back to the Premier League.

Tom Heaton, Ben Mee and Scott Arfield played in each and every one of the 46 league games while Michael Keane, George Boyd, Sam Vokes, David Jones and Andre Gray all topped 40 appearances, with Joey Barton just two short of that tally.

Gray proved to be worth every penny of the big fee invested in him the previous summer. The former Brentford hot-shot finished as the top scorer in the division with 23 league goals and a couple more in the cup for good measure.

The biggest win of the season was a 5-0 thumping of MK Dons on their own turf, the start of a purple patch that brought a dozen goals in three games. However the success of the side was based on solidity at the back. A measly 35 goals were conceded in 46 league games providing the rock on which a goal difference of plus 37 was achieved from a season that concluded with just five defeats and 26 victories.

The last two against QPR and Charlton Athletic being the games that brought the glory, but the hard work had been done week in week out all season.

21

BURNLEY FOOTBALL CLUB
sky BET CHAMPIONSHIP
CHAMPIONS 2016
BURNLEY

FOOTBALL LEA
CHAMPI

sky BET CHAMPIONSHIP
CHAMPIONS 2015/16

HERE WE GO!

Joey Barton's winner away to Preston left Sean Dyche's men knowing that just one more win was required to mathematically ensure promotion and there were two games to achieve it. 19,362 packed into Turf Moor to see the Clarets do it at home to QPR where the man to thank was Sam Vokes.

Nerves were beginning to jangle as everyone tried to will a winner. Midway through the first half Vokes' shot had appeared to hit the hand of Rangers' defender Cole Kpekawa but no penalty was forthcoming. An hour had gone when the magic moment came. Vokes was first to David Jones' free-kick as he scored the all important goal with his flicked on header. With 10 minutes to go Vokes had the ball in the net again only to have his effort ruled out but when the final whistle blew 1-0 was enough and Burnley were back.

A glance at that night's league table may have raised doubts as Burnley were just two points ahead of Middlesbrough and Brighton with a game to play but with those two nearest challengers still to face each other they couldn't both get three points and so Burnley had done it.

In the end the title was secured with a four point winning margin. Goals from Vokes, George Boyd and the division's top scorer Andre Gray sealed a 3-0 win at already relegated Charlton Athletic whose boss Jose Riga resigned after the match. While the Addicks fans were restless, the travelling fans were buoyant even though they had to wait until a civic reception back in Burnley to see the trophy presented.

For Sean Dyche and his team it was the culmination of a superb season where the only defeat suffered since Boxing Day had been a narrow 2-1 FA Cup reverse away to holders Arsenal.

Skills: Cruyff Turn

1 Draw back your foot as if you are going to kick the ball

2 Instead of following through, stop your foot over the ball...

3 ...and push it back behind your other leg while starting to turn your body.

4 Finish turning through 180° and head in the opposite direction.

5 Your unsuspecting opponent will be left standing wondering what just happened!

Johan Cruyff debuted his signature dummy at the 1974 FIFA World Cup. The trick is a brilliant manoeuvre to fool your opponent and change direction.

Sam Vokes

Here is the first half of our Premier League A-Z. The answer to each clue begins with the corresponding letter of the alphabet.

A-Z OF THE

A — Captained Arsenal to the European Cup Winners' Cup win in 1994

B

C — Crystal Palace's all-time top appearance maker

D — He scored two goals in Swansea's 5-0 League Cup final win over Bradford in 2013

E — He spent a successful seven-year spell at Chelsea

F — Man City retired squad number 23 in memory of this player

G — Burnley's top scorer last season

Hull City played their home games here before moving to the KC Stadium

26

PREMIER LEAGUE

H — Led Bournemouth to promotion to the Premier League last season

I — Meaning of the latin phrase 'Consectatio Excellentiae' on Sunderland's crest

J — Honorary life president of Watford FC

K — Man City's Belgian captain

L — Man U have won the FA Cup 12 times, this man scored the winner in the 2016 final

M — Manager of Boro when they won the League Cup in 2004

ANSWERS ON PAGE 62

Professional footballers at top level can run around 12 kilometres per game...

Quite often, they might have to play two matches within three or four days of each other and over the course of a season, regular players could play in the region of 50 games!

That would be a lot if they were simply running as a long distance runner does. In football though, that running is done with a mixture of short sprints from a standing start and runs of various lengths at differing intensities. On top of this, there is a lot of twisting and turning, often while someone is trying to pull the player back or even kick them. If they can cope with this, there is then the consideration that once the footballer has the ball, they have to use it, either with a telling pass or a shot on goal, while the opposition do all they can to stop them. Added to this is the fact that the thousands of fans watching in the stadium and the millions viewing on TV are only too ready to criticise them if they do not get it right.

To cope with all this, players have to be supremely fit so they have the stamina to last 90 minutes on a regular basis, and have the competitive edge to deal with opponents trying to stop them.

Players also have to be careful to eat and drink the right things, ge the right amount of sleep and keep themselves in tip-top shape.

In the summer when players return from a few weeks off, they do a lot of physical training to get themselves ready for the big kick-off. Once a few games have been played and they have, what players call, 'match-fitness', their aim is to maintain that fitness, but not over-do things.

Most players will train for two or three hours most days and do additional work in the gym, as well as perhaps doing pilates or yoga to help look after their bodies. Cycling and swimming can be useful too, but so is knowing when to simply rest, because the Premier League season is a long and gruelling campaign.

28

PRE-SEASON TRAINING

Andre Gray

ON THE ROAD

Can you figure out where every team in the Premier League plays their home games? Fill in the missing words and find all the grounds in the grid!

Team	Ground	Team	Ground	Team	Ground
Arsenal	_____ Stadium	Leicester	King _____ Stadium	Sunderland	Stadium of _____
Bournemouth	_____ Stadium	Liverpool	_____	Swansea	_____ Stadium
Burnley	____ Moor	Man City	_____ Stadium	Tottenham	_____ Hart _____
Chelsea	_____ Bridge	Man United	Old _____	Watford	_____ Road
Crystal Palace	_____ Park	Middlesbrough	_____ Stadium	West Brom	The _____
Everton	_____ Park	Southampton	St ____'s Stadium	West Ham	_____ Stadium
Hull	KC _____	Stoke	_____ Stadium		

ANSWERS ON PAGE 62

DANGER MEN

ARSENAL
LUCAS PEREZ

Signed from Deportivo La Coruna for a reported £17m just before the closure of the transfer window, 'Lucas' is a good fit for the Gunners. A player who looks to play 'one-two's' in and around the box the 28-year-old has played in Ukraine and Greece as well as Spain. Barcelona and Atletico Madrid were amongst his victims as he struck 18 times in 37 games last season, the best of his career so far.

BURNLEY
ANDRE GRAY

Having fired Burnley back into the Premier League in his first season at Turf Moor, 25-year-old Gray showed he intended to carry on in fine style in the Premier League with an early season goal in a sensational win over Liverpool. Wolverhampton born Andre came to the Clarets via Brentford who he'd joined after his goals brought Luton Town back into the Football League.

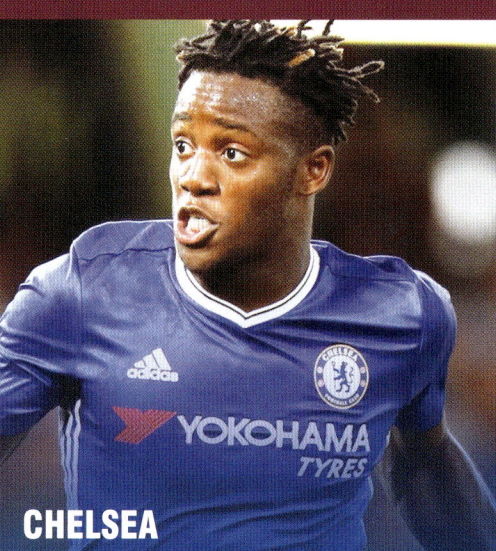

BOURNEMOUTH
CALLUM WILSON

Speed merchant Wilson made his name with his hometown team Coventry, costing the Cherries £3m in 2014. Having helped them into the Premier League he hit an early season hat-trick against West Ham but then picked up an injury which ruined his season. This time round he is hoping to show his Bourne supremacy.

CHELSEA
MICHY BATSHUAYI

Antonio Conte made Michy his first signing for the Blues, splashing out £33m on the young Belgium international. Strong and quick, Batshuayi could be Stamford Bridge's new Didier Drogba and like Drogba lists Marseille as one of his previous clubs. He also impressed with Standard Liege and is excellent at linking up play as well as putting the ball into the back of the net.

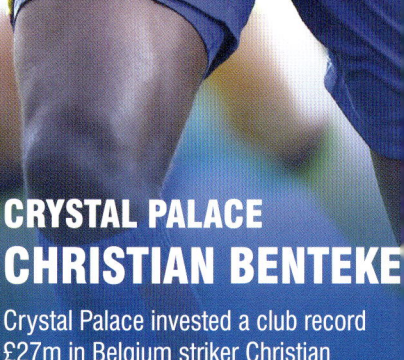

CRYSTAL PALACE
CHRISTIAN BENTEKE

Crystal Palace invested a club record £27m in Belgium striker Christian Benteke in the summer, potential add-ons possibly adding another £5m to that fee. Class costs and the Eagles have a top class forward in Benteke who after beginning in Belgian football scored 49 goals in 101 games for Aston Villa before a £32.5m move to Liverpool where he netted 10 times in 42 games.

Watch out for these dangermen when the Clarets meet their Premier League rivals...

EVERTON
ROMELU LUKAKU

Still only 23, Lukaku is a powerhouse striker and probably the nearest thing in the game to his boyhood hero Didier Drogba. Romelu emulated his idol by making Chelsea his first English club. A debutant with Anderlecht when he had just turned 16, he excelled on loan from Chelsea to West Brom and subsequently moved to Everton, the Toffees making him their record signing at £28m. For Belgium he had scored 14 goals in 49 games at the start of this season.

LIVERPOOL
SADIO MANE

The scorer of the quickest hat-trick in Premier League history when he took just 2 minutes 56 seconds to net three times for Southampton against Aston Villa in 2015! The Senegal international speed merchant cost Liverpool £34m last summer, shortly after he'd scored twice against them, quickly followed by a hat-trick against Manchester City.

HULL CITY
DIEUMERCI MBOKANI

Signed just as the transfer window closed in the summer on loan from Dynamo Kiev, Mbokani came to Hull with experience of the Premier League having scored seven times on loan to Norwich last season. The 31-year-old Zaire international has played in five countries and won six league titles and as many cups.

LEICESTER CITY
JAMIE VARDY

Jamie Vardy is the reigning Footballer of the Year and Premier League Player of the Year. His hard work and dedication has seen him rise from non-league football to the dizzy heights of the Premier League. Last season he helped fire Leicester City to the top of the table and himself into the England team.

MANCHESTER CITY
SERGIO AGUERO

As dangerous as any dangerman in the Premier League 'Kun' Aguero is simply a goal machine. He's fired City to two Premier League titles and two League Cups and started this season with six goals in his first three games including a Champions League hat-trick. Last season his haul included a hat-trick against Chelsea and five goals in a blistering 20 minute spell against relegation bound Newcastle.

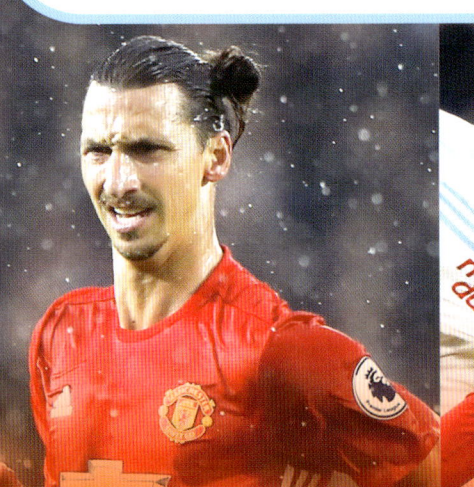

Watch out for these dangermen when the Clarets meet their Premier League rivals...

MANCHESTER UNITED
ZLATAN IBRAHIMOVIC

There are many stars in the Premier League and Zlatan Ibrahimovic is as big as any of them. The Super-Swede has finally arrived in English football this season after playing in the Netherlands, Italy, Spain and France as well as his own country. He has won the league title in 12 of his last 13 seasons and had scored 392 goals in 677 games at the start of this season.

SOUTHAMPTON
SOFIANE BOUFAL

Southampton broke their transfer record to bring in 22-year-old Morocco international attacking midfielder Sofiane Boufal shortly before the summer transfer window closed. Boufal began his career with Angers and came to the fore last season with Lille where he played in the final of the French League Cup against PSG a week after scoring a brilliant hat-trick against Ajaccio.

MIDDLESBROUGH
ALVARO NEGREDO

A debut goal on the opening day of the season is likely to be the first of many for the man who, when at Manchester City, bagged hat-tricks in the Champions League and the semi-final of the League Cup. In between his spells in England, Negredo played for Valencia, a team he once scored four goals in a game against for Sevilla.

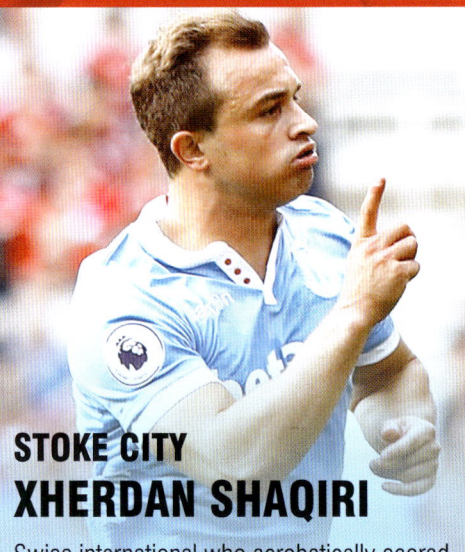

STOKE CITY
XHERDAN SHAQIRI

Swiss international who acrobatically scored one of the most spectacular goals at Euro 16 against Poland. Having won three league titles and a cup at the start of his career with FC Basel in Switzerland, he moved on to Bayern Munich with whom he won the Champions League in 2013, as well as the European Super Cup, the World Club Cup and two Bundesliga titles before moving on to another continental giant in Inter Milan before coming to Stoke.

SUNDERLAND
JERMAIN DEFOE

Harry Kane and Jamie Vardy were the only English players to score more Premier League goals than Defoe last season. Jermain's tally of 15 included a hat-trick at Swansea when he claimed his second match ball of the campaign having also scored three in a League Cup tie with Exeter. At the start of this season Jermain was the last player to score a hat-trick for England and he will be looking for a return to the international fold now that his ex-Sunderland manager Sam Allardyce has taken over the national side.

SWANSEA CITY
BORJA BASTON

Swansea spent £15.5m in August to bring in Spanish striker Borja Baston. Last season he ripped up la Liga with 18 goals in 29 starts and seven sub appearances with Eibar, including a goal away to Barcelona. In 2009 Baston won the Golden Boot by scoring five goals at the U17 World Cup and now he'll look to fulfil his potential in the Prem.

WEST BROMWICH ALBION
SALOMON RONDON

After taking time to get used to life in the Premier League, Venezuela international Salomon Rondon really looked to be getting to grips with the demands of English football by the end of his first season. Having come to Europe as a teenager in 2008 when he moved to Las Palmas his ability as a dangerman has since seen Malaga break their club record for him with Rubin Kazan investing £10m, Zenit St Petersburg a whopping £15.8m and West Brom a record £12m!

WATFORD
ODION IGHALO

Famed for his 'picture-goals' Odion has been with the Hornets since 2014. He scored 20 goals in his first season as Watford won promotion and scored 15 (plus a couple in the cups) in his first season in the Premier League when he won the League's Player of the Month award in December 2015. A Nigerian international, Ighalo played in Nigeria, Norway, Italy and Spain before coming to England.

TOTTENHAM HOTSPUR
HARRY KANE

The Premier League's top scorer in 2015/16 with 25 goals, Kane bagged 21 the year before (31 in all competitions). Now 23, Harry debuted for Tottenham in 2011 in a Europa League game with Hearts before loans with Leyton Orient, Millwall, Norwich and Leicester helped him develop his game. Now one of the most feared strikers in the league Kane started the season with five goals in 16 games for England.

WEST HAM UNITED
SIMONE ZAZA

Italy international Simone Zaza is on a year's loan to the Hammers who have the option of signing the 25-year-old from Juventus for a fee that would total over 20m Euros. Although infamous for his flamboyantly fluffed penalty against Germany at Euro 2016, Zaza is a real dangerman because as well as offering pace and strength he is also a threat in the air.

Put your creative talents to the test...

DESIGN A NEW KIT

Scott Arfield

Can you figure out the identity of these Burnley stars?

Who are yer?

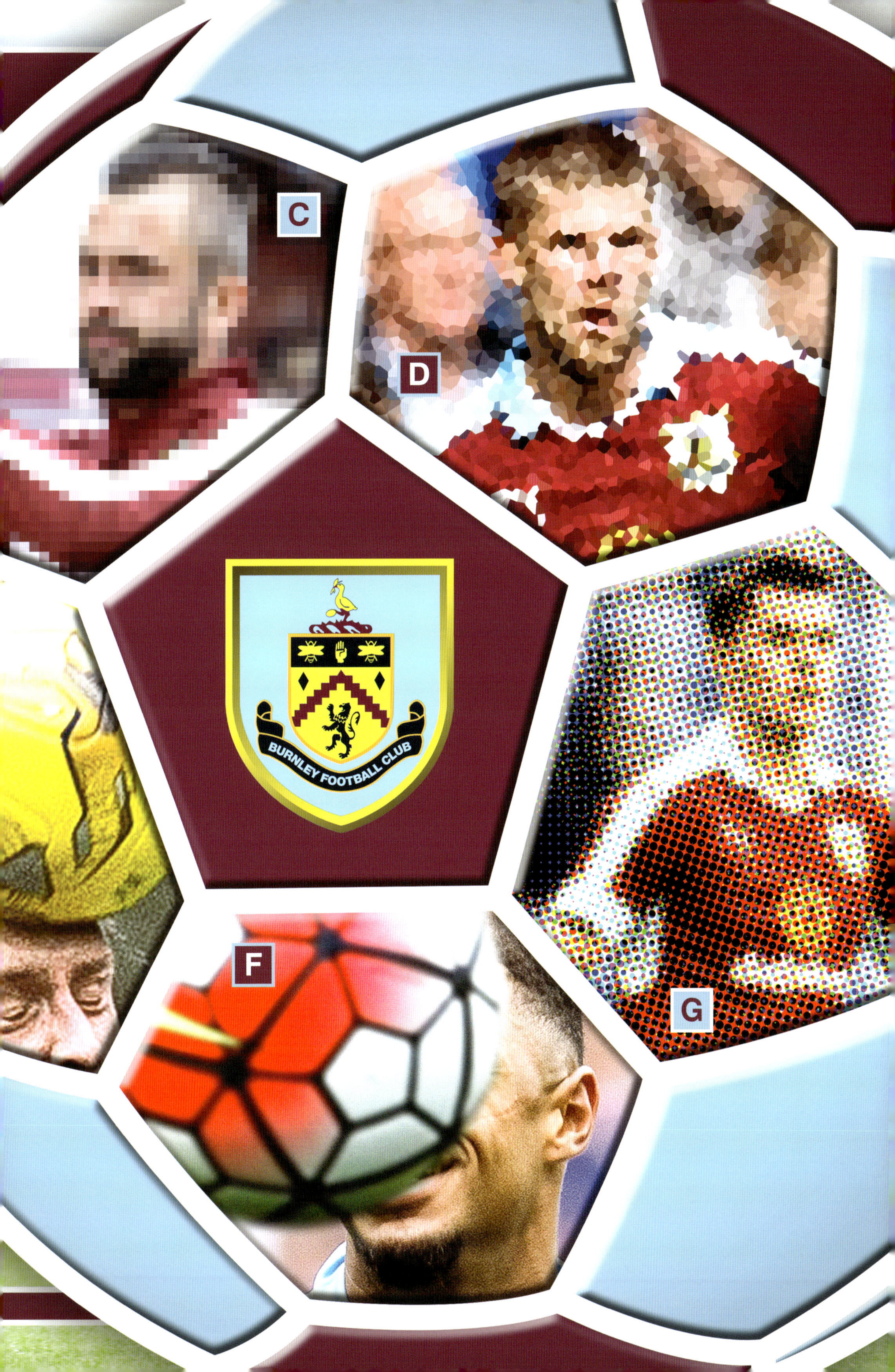
C
D
BURNLEY FOOTBALL CLUB
F
G

JOHN ANGUS

A loyal servant at Turf Moor from 1955 to 1972, right-back John made 439 league appearances, being ever present in 1962/63. A year earlier he'd been a runner-up in both league and cup but gained a winner's medal in the 1960 title success.

ALEX ELDER

Club captain at Burnley this Northern Ireland international left-back won the league at Turf Moor in 1960 and reached the cup final two years later.

JIMMY ADAMSON

Footballer of the Year in 1962 when he captained Burnley at Wembley, Jimmy went on to coach England at the World Cup that summer. In 1960 he was skipper as the club won the league. He later managed Burnley.

COLIN McDONALD

Voted the best goalkeeper at the 1958 World Cup, Colin won eight England caps while with Burnley. After 186 league appearances for the Clarets, Colin's career was ended when he broke his leg representing the Football League.

BRIAN MILLER

An England international centre-half who never missed a game as Burnley won the league title in 1960. Brian was with the club from 1954 until 1968, he later had two spells as manager.

JOHN CONNELLY

A title winner with Burnley and Manchester United, this England international winger scored a highly impressive 86 goals in 215 league games for the Clarets for whom he was also a cup finalist in 1962.

DREAM

ANDRE GRAY

JIMMY McILROY
Selected for a Great Britain team in 1955, Jimmy won his first Northern Ireland cap when still a teenager. He won the league and reached the cup final while at Turf Moor, he played over 500 games and also became President of the club.

MARTIN DOBSON
Classy midfielder who always seemed to have time on the ball. Martin captained Burnley to titles in the second and third division in 1973 and 1982. An England international, he commanded a British transfer record of £300,000 when sold to Everton in 1974.

LEIGHTON JAMES
A product of the famous Turf Moor youth system, James was a feisty left winger who regularly delivered the most deliciously inviting crosses. Capped 23 times by Wales.

RAY POINTER
Ever-present when Burnley were league champions in 1960. Ray scored 118 times in 223 Clarets league games and played in the 1962 FA Cup final. He was also an England international.

Big money buy in 2015, striker Gray was an instant success, firing Burnley back into the Premier League with 23 goals (plus two for Brentford) making him the 2015/16 Championship Player of the Year and Golden Boot winner.

25
JohannBerg Gudmundsson

Can you work out in which season each of these photos was taken?
There's a clue to help you with each one!

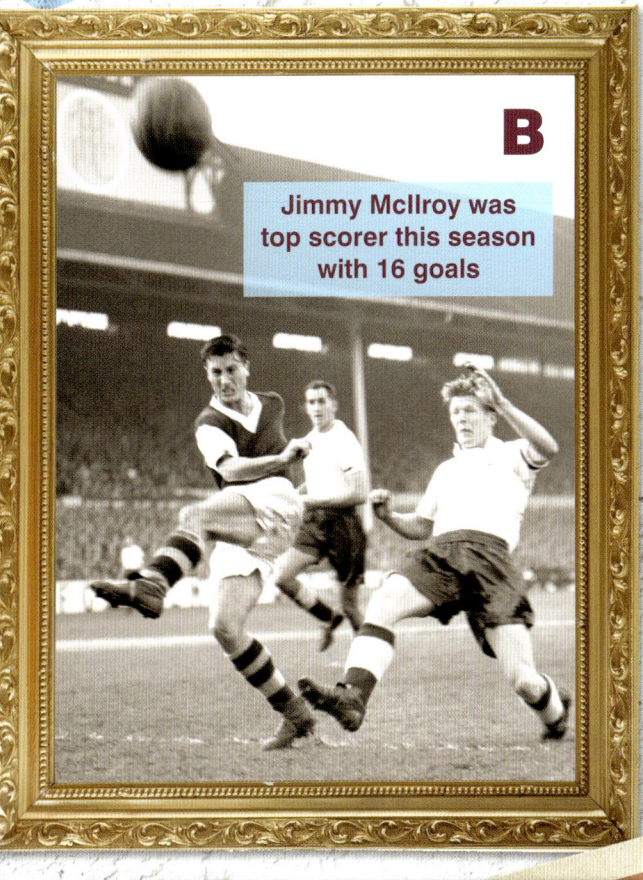

Spot the Season

A — Glen Little was Burnley's number 7 this season

B — Jimmy McIlroy was top scorer this season with 16 goals

C — Burnley players met HRH the Duke of Gloucester this season

D — This was Stan Ternent's first season in charge

E — Ralph Coates was well into his Burnley career at this point. The pitch is a sign of the times!

ANSWERS ON PAGE 62

Here is the second half of our Premier League A-Z.

The answer to each clue begins with the corresponding letter of the alphabet.

A-Z OF THE

N — West Ham's captain

O — Leicester's manager when they last won the League Cup in 2000

P — West Brom's first summer signing

Q —

R — The manager who led the Foxes to the Premier League title

S — Captain of Stoke City

— Signed to Sunderland as a striker and later became the club's chairman

44

PREMIER LEAGUE

T — Everton's nickname

U — Tottenham's kit manufacturer

V — Stoke played their home games here before moving to the Britannia Stadium in 1997

W — Southampton's anthem

X — Arsenal's first summer signing

Y — Liverpool's club motto

Z — Chelsea's player of the year in 2003

ANSWERS ON PAGE 62

Skills: Rainbow Kick

1 Start off with your feet on either side of the ball

2 Use one foot to roll the ball up your other leg

3 Make sure to roll the ball hard enough to give it some air

4 When the ball is in the air strike it with your heel

5 ...and flick it over your head!

Brazilian star striker, Neymar, is well known for his use of the rainbow kick on the pitch and regularly fools his opposition. The trick is an impressive show of skill which takes practise, practise practise!

46   TIP: Lean forward as you're doing the trick, this helps create space between you and the ball so you can strike it more easily.

Michael Keane

05

There are five members of Team GB hidden in the crowd.

FANTASTIC

Can you find them all?

ANSWERS ON PAGE 62

49

AIDEN O'NEILL

Burnley's very own Wizard of Oz, talented Australian midfielder Aiden O'Neill looks all set to grab the opportunity handed to him by boss Sean Dyche and make his mark on the Clarets' 2016/17 Premier League campaign.

The Brisbane-born 18-year-old began his youth career with Brisbane Athletic before moving to England aged just 16 to pursue his ultimate dream of playing in the Premier League.

O'Neill had to endure something of a frustrating time when he first arrived at Turf Moor as the club worked hard behind the scenes to obtain the necessary international clearance. However, O'Neill wasted little time in impressing all at the training ground with both his attitude and ability.

With a real appetite to receive the ball, and always looking to make things happen, O'Neill played for both the youth team and development squad in 2015/16. He signed his first professional contract in January 2016.

His first team breakthrough arrived at the start of the 2016/17 campaign on what proved to be a memorable afternoon for the club and the player himself. With the Clarets leading 2-0 against Liverpool, in only the second Premier League fixture of the season, boss Dyche handed O'Neill his debut as the youngster replaced goalscorer Andre Gray in the closing stages of what was a memorable victory for the team at Turf Moor.

The highly promising youngster followed up his first team bow against Liverpool with a first start four days later in the League Cup tie away to Accrington Stanley. A player who has clearly made his mark on the Burnley management team - Aiden O'Neill is certainly a young man with a bright future ahead of him and clearly one to watch over the coming weeks and months.

wonderkid

GOAL OF THE SEASON

Scott Arfield's strike against Blackburn Rovers was voted the club's goal of the season.

Arfield picked the perfect moment to score his first goal of the campaign and settle the derby day spoils.

The Clarets wide man found the top corner in the 62nd minute with a wonderfully precise strike to seal a second successive win at Ewood Park and assured himself of hero status in Burnley.

And just how much it meant to the Scot was evident as he sparked joyous scenes, racing 80 yards, pursued by his teammates, to celebrate his matchwinner with over 4,500 travelling Clarets fans.

"It is a controlled finish, it's all about technique, a fantastic goal worthy of winning any game," commented his very happy manager Sean Dyche.

A

Jimmy Mullen celebrates with the trophy after victory in the Division Two Play-offs

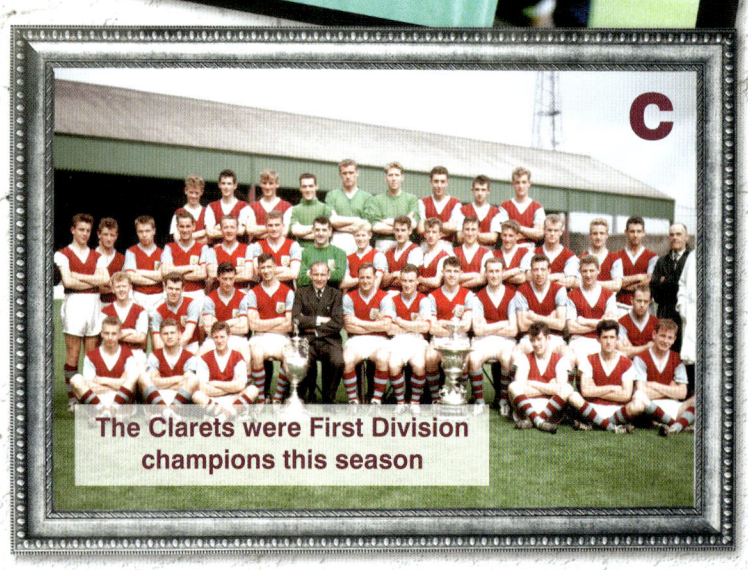

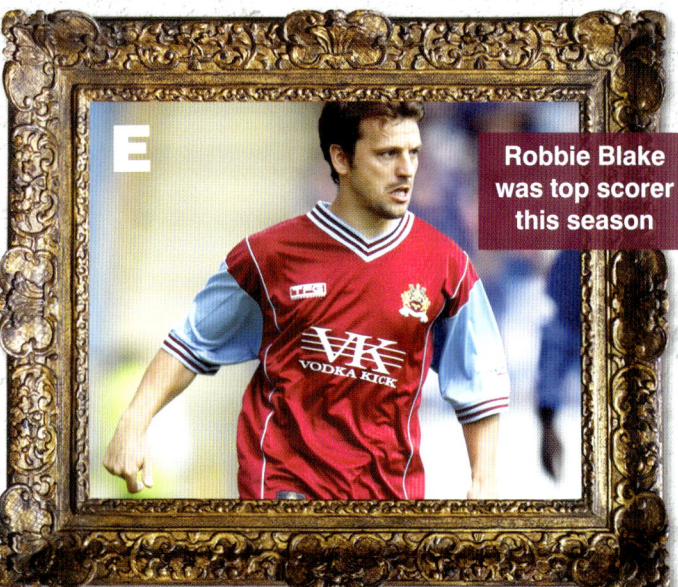

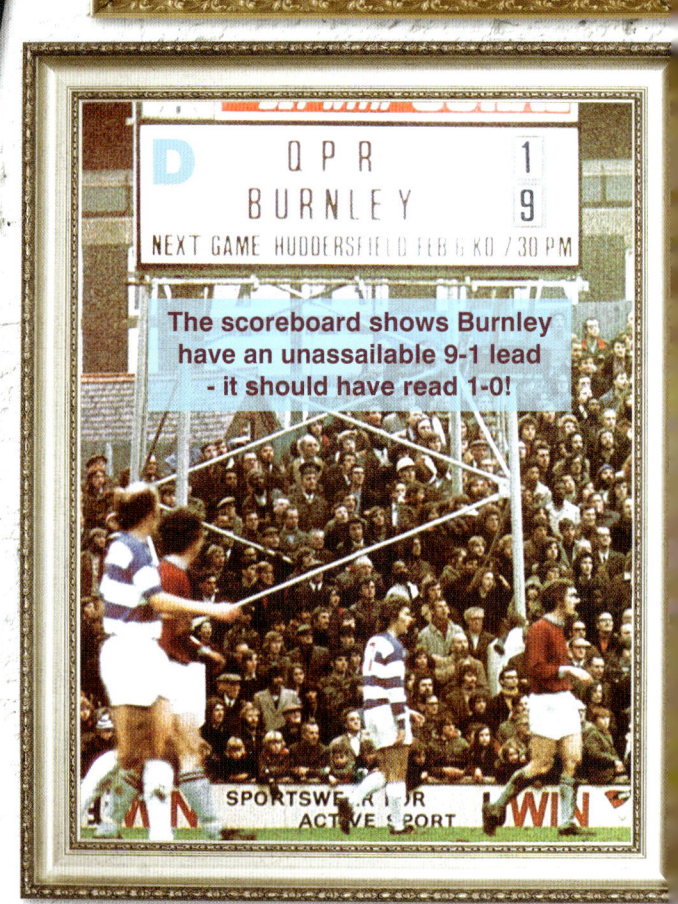

Can you work out in which season each of these photos was taken?
There's a clue to help you with each one!

B

All-time top appearance maker Jerry Dawson signed for Burnley this season

C

The Clarets were First Division champions this season

D

The scoreboard shows Burnley have an unassailable 9-1 lead – it should have read 1-0!

E

Robbie Blake was top scorer this season

Spot the season

52 ANSWERS ON PAGE 6

Jeff Hendrick

13

BEN MEE

Mee was an integral part of last season's Championship title success as he made 49 appearances and was voted Player's Player of the Year by his teammates.

The Clarets kept 20 clean sheets during the 2015/16 season, with the Manchester City Academy graduate moving into a centre-back role in December alongside Michael Keane.

The Sale-born defender signed permanently in 2012 after an initial loan spell from Manchester City, where he captained their 2008 FA Youth Cup winning squad, and signed a new three-year deal with the Clarets this summer.

He has forged a reputation as a brave and fearless operator, helping the Claret to promotion in 2013/14 before making 33 Premier League appearances, which included a dramatic equaliser in the 1-1 draw against Chelsea, the following season. And ahead of another tilt at the top-flight, the 26-year-old is confident that the club can continue to move forward. Mee said:

"This club is going somewhere the minute. It's been ever-changing throughout my time here and you can see the things going on at the training ground and the way the team is going.

"It's exciting and we're definitely moving forwards. Now I just want to help keep the team in the Premier League. That's my short-term goal and I want to be a big part of it.

"There's a togetherness and a will to do well and I am sure that will stand us in good stead."

PLAYERS' PLAYER OF THE YEAR

What Ball?

A

B

There are too many footballs! Work out which is the real ball in each photo.

ANSWERS ON PAGE 62

55

CLUB OR COUNTRY?

Can you work out which set of clues is pointing to... they could be Premier League, Championship or international

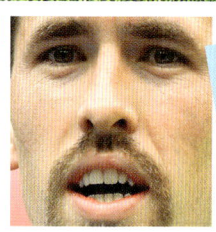

1.
2. 
3. 
4.
5. 
6. 
7. 
8. 
9. 

ANSWERS ON PAGE 62

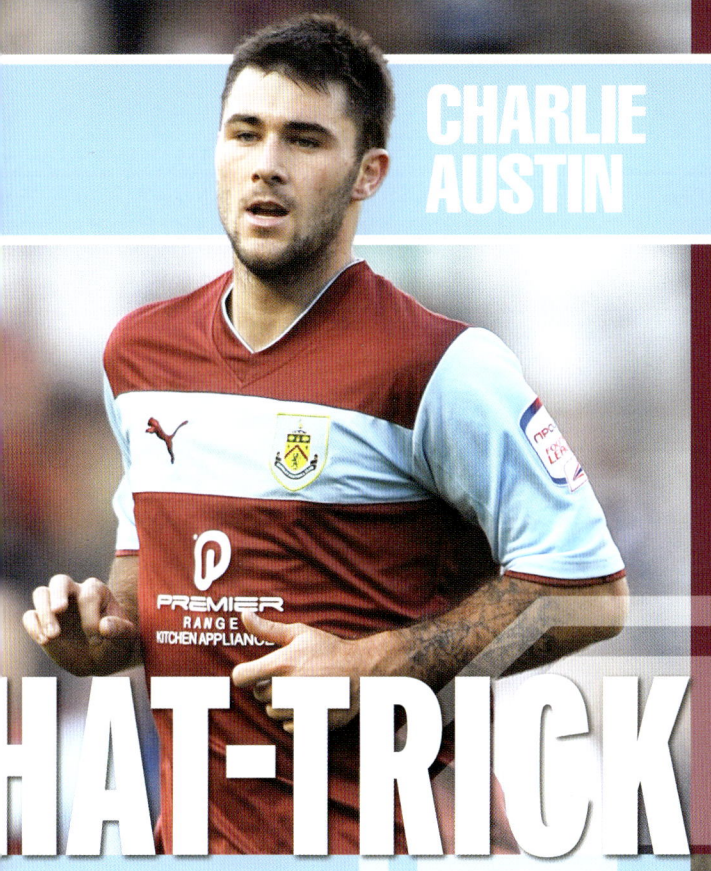

CHARLIE AUSTIN

There's very little to put a smile on a striker's face more than scoring a hat-trick in a winning performance. Take a look back at three special Clarets trebles...

Burnley 3-3 Sheffield Wednesday
2 October 2012

Charlie Austin's third hat-trick of 2012 strangely brought only one point whereas the previous ones had been part of five goal hauls in big wins over Portsmouth and Peterborough. Taking home a third match ball of the calendar year showed just what a prolific striker Austin was, this hat-trick gave the marksman 14 goals from 11 games, making him the country's leading scorer.

Before the evening kick-off it was pouring at Turf Moor and for the 12,000 who attended it was soon raining goals. Three times Charlie gave Eddie Howe's side the lead, the first two before half-time with well-taken headers, the third with a brilliant shot from just outside the box six minutes from time.

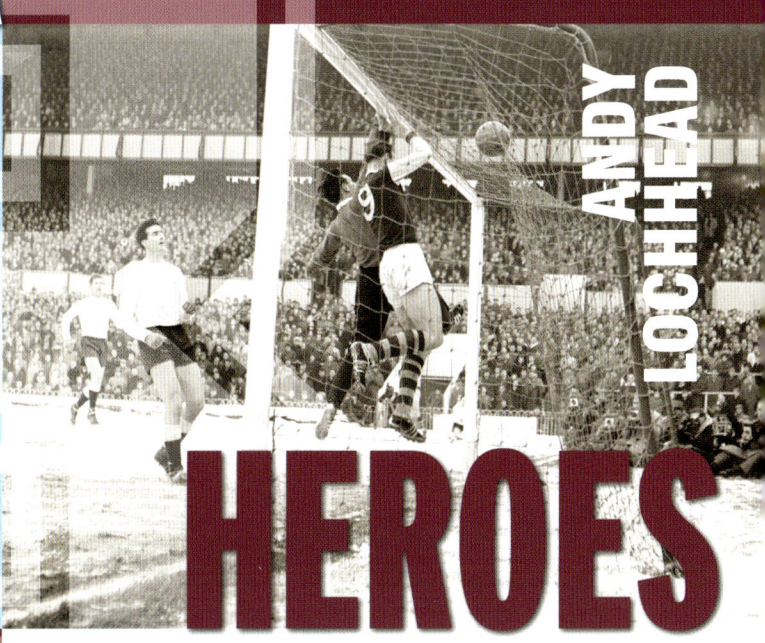

HAT-TRICK

Burnley 6-1 Manchester United
26 December 1963

When Clarets fans woke up on Boxing Day 1963 little did they know they were going to have even more to bring cheer than when they had opened their Christmas presents 24 hours earlier. FA Cup holders Manchester United were four points off the top of the table but were destroyed at Turf Moor with centre forward Andy Lochhead scoring four goals.

Scottish striker Andy is still a matchday host at Burnley. This was one of seven hat-tricks he scored for the club for whom he twice scored five times in a game.

United goalkeeper David Gaskell wasn't the only goalkeeper to have backache that day as a record 66 goals were scored in the ten top-flight games played that day!

ANDY LOCHHEAD

HEROES

TOM NICOL

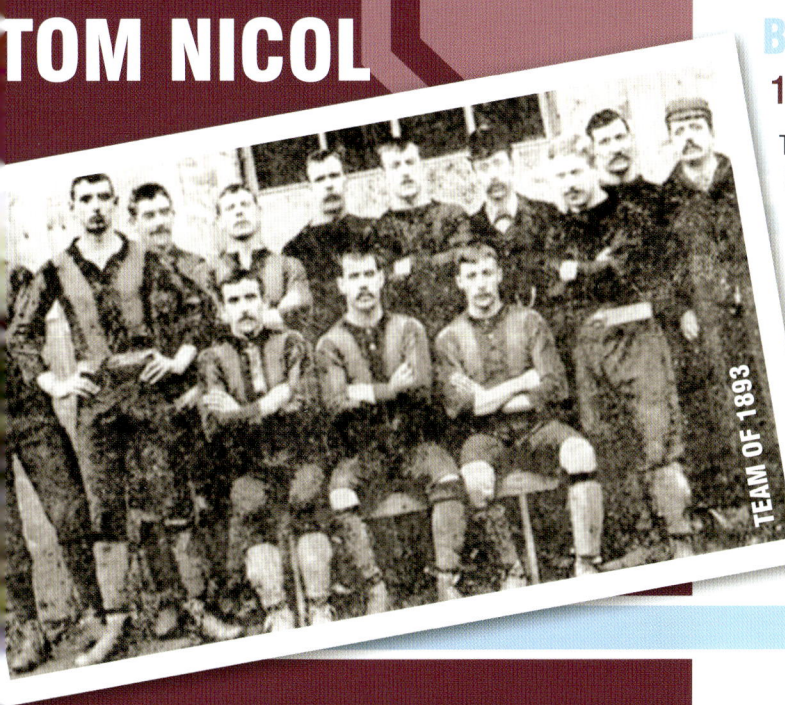

Burnley 6-0 Blackburn Rovers
13 April 1896

Tom Nicol had hit a debut hat-trick against Preston North End and been on the mark in Burnley's first ever win over Blackburn in 1891 but in 1896 Tom bagged the only Burnley hat-trick in the Cotton Mills derby as Rovers were routed to the tune of 6-0!

Blackburn obviously couldn't forget the damage Nicol had done to them as they signed him the following November. Evidently there was space in their line up as John Yarwood and James Parkinson made their debuts in their historic hammering - and never played for them again!

Nicol was a Scotsman who spent two of his seasons with Burnley playing as a full-back. He also played as a winger but was more than useful as a centre-forward.

TEAM OF 1893

Skills: Maradona Spin

1 Start off by simply dribbling the ball

2 While moving in a forward motion, tap the ball with your leading foot...

3 ...and start turning your body in the opposite direction

4

5 As you're spinning, pull the ball back with your other foot while continuing to turn

6 Then keep moving forward!

Argentinian maestro, Maradona, is very well known for this move. It is brilliant for overcoming opponents and getting yourself into space, as while you are spinning you are putting your back to the defender and shielding the ball.

Steven Defour

What do you think will happen in 2017? 2016/17

PREMIER LEAGUE

PREDICTION FOR PREMIER LEAGUE WINNERS:
Manchester Utd

YOUR PREDICTION:

PREDICTION FOR PREMIER LEAGUE RUNNERS-UP:
Chelsea

YOUR PREDICTION:

THE CHAMPIONSHIP

PREDICTION FOR CHAMPIONSHIP WINNERS:
Norwich City

YOUR PREDICTION:

PREDICTION FOR ALSO PROMOTED TO THE PREMIER LEAGUE:
Derby County & Brighton & HA

YOUR PREDICTION:

PREDICTIONS

THE FA CUP

PREDICTION FOR FA CUP WINNERS:
Burnley

YOUR PREDICTION:

PREDICTION FOR FA CUP FINALISTS:
Liverpool

YOUR PREDICTION:

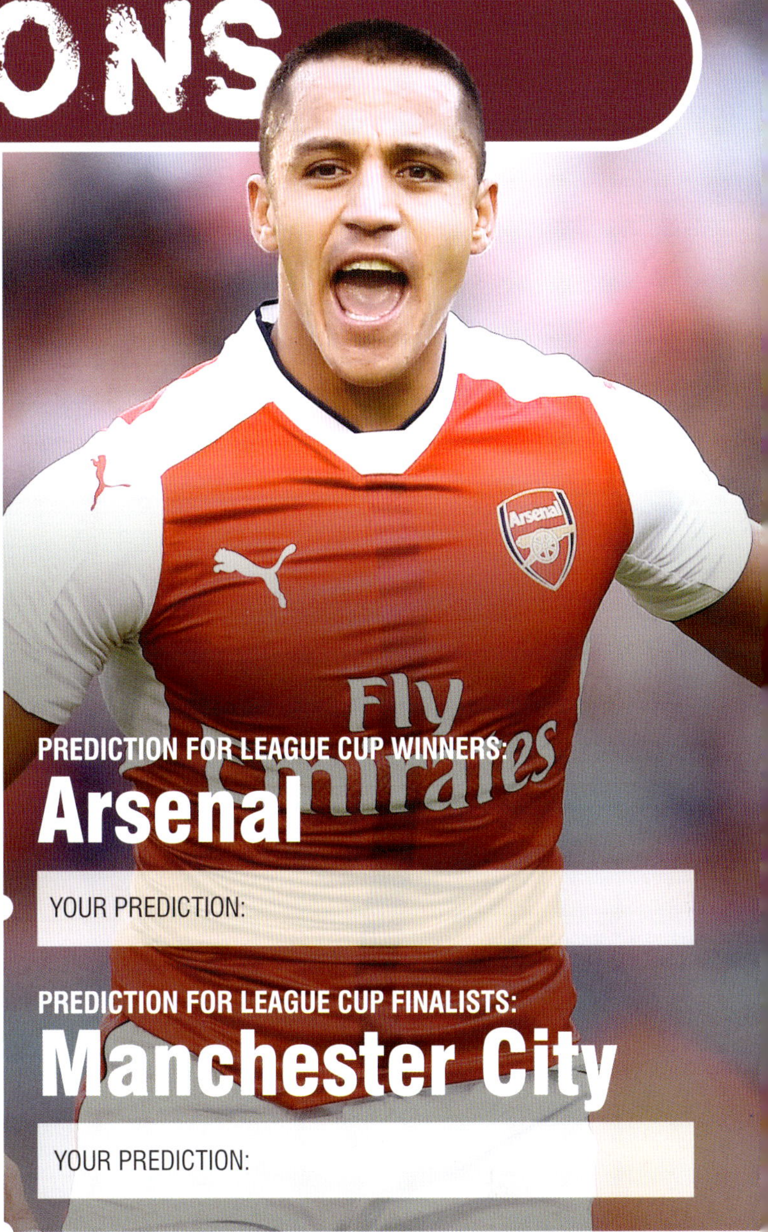

PREDICTION FOR LEAGUE CUP WINNERS:
Arsenal

YOUR PREDICTION:

PREDICTION FOR LEAGUE CUP FINALISTS:
Manchester City

YOUR PREDICTION:

THE LEAGUE CUP

ANSWERS

PAGE 19 · SPOT THE SEASON
a. 1913/14, b. 2013/14, c. 1991/92, d. 1974/75, e. 1961/62.

PAGE 26 · A-Z OF THE PREMIER LEAGUE
a. Tony Adams, b. Boothferry Park, c. Jim Cannon, d. Nathan Dyer, e. Michael Essien, f. Marc-Vivien Foe, g. Andre Gray, h. Eddie Howe, i. In pursuit of excellence, j. Sir Elton John, k. Vincent Kompany, l. Jesse Lingard, m. Steve McClaren.

PAGE 31 · ON THE ROAD
Arsenal - Emirates Stadium, Bournemouth - Vitality Stadium, Burnley - Turf Moor, Chelsea - Stamford Bridge, Crystal Palace - Selhurst Park, Everton - Goodison Park, Hull - KC Stadium, Leicester - King Power Stadium, Liverpool - Anfield, Man City - Etihad Stadium, Man United - Old Trafford, Middlesbrough - Riverside Stadium, Southampton - St Mary's Stadium, Stoke - bet365 Stadium, Sunderland - Stadium of Light, Swansea - Liberty Stadium, Tottenham - White Hart Lane, Watford - Vicarage Road, West Brom - The Hawthorns, West Ham - London Stadium.

PAGE 38 · WHO ARE YER?
a. Stephen Ward, b. Matt Lowton, c. Steven Defour, d. Johann Berg Gudmundsson, e. Ben Mee, f. Michael Keane, g. Andre Gray.

PAGE 43 · SPOT THE SEASON
a. 2001/02, b.1956/57, c.1946/47, d. 1998/99, e. 1968/69.

PAGE 44 · A-Z OF THE PREMIER LEAGUE
n. Mark Noble, o. Martin O'Neill, p. Matt Phillips, q. Niall Quinn, r. Claudio Ranieri, s. Ryan Shawcross, t. the Toffees, u. Under Armour, v. Victoria Ground, w. When the Saints go marching in, x. Granit Xhaka, y. You'll never walk alone, z. Gianfranco Zola.

PAGE 48 · FANTASTIC
Bradley Wiggins, Nicola Adams, Andy Murray, Jessica Ennis-Hill and Greg Rutherford.

PAGE 52 · SPOT THE SEASON
a. 1993/94, b. 1906/07, c. 1959/60, d. 1982/73, e. 2003/04.

PAGE 55 · WHAT BALL?
Picture A - Ball 8, Picture B - Ball 1.

PAGE 56 · CLUB OR COUNTRY?
1. Hull City, 2. Newcastle United, 3. Spain, 4.Austria, 5. Wigan Athletic, 6. Tottenham Hotspur, 7. Iceland, 8. Arsenal, 9. Wolverhampton Wanderers.